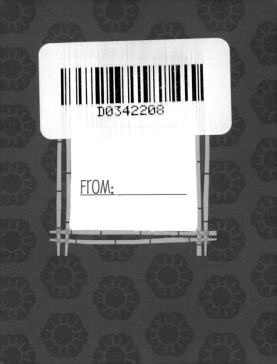

D0342208

FROM: _____

# FENG SHOE

## BY LAO SHU

"Translated" by Michael W. Domis

Illustrated by Amy Saidens

PETER PAUPER PRESS, INC.
White Plains, New York

For Miss Jessica Allen,
because she wears wrestling shoes,
and makes them look good

Illustrations copyright © 2004
Amy Saidens/www.artscounselinc.com

Designed by Taryn R. Sefecka

Copyright © 2004
Peter Pauper Press, Inc.
202 Mamaroneck Avenue
White Plains, NY 10601

ISBN 978-1-59359-952-2
Printed in China
14  13  12

Visit us at www.peterpauper.com

# CONTENTS

Introduction . . . . . . . . . . . . . . . . . . . . . 6

Chapter the First—
    The Basics of Feng Shoe . . . . . . . . . 8

Chapter the Second—Shoe Styles . . . 18

Chapter the Third—Shoe Storage . . . 31

Chapter the Fourth—
    Shoe Shopping . . . . . . . . . . . . . . . . 44

Chapter the Fifth—
    Shoe Makers and Their Craft . . . . . 58

Chapter the Sixth—
    Famous Feng Shoe-isms . . . . . . . . 66

Chapter the Seventh—Shu-ku . . . . . 71

A Final Thought from Lao Shu . . . . . . 79

# INTRODUCTION

The book you're holding is a translation of an ancient text of Lao Shu, Foot Philosopher to the Empress. We find the advice in the book to be just as relevant today as it was 824 years ago. Choosing the correct shoe can encourage good fortune, a propitious lifestyle, love, wealth, and good health. By placing well-made and fashionably appointed footwear on your feet, you can ensure the maximum flow of positive *ch'i* (life force) throughout your body. By following the advice of the

Foot Philosopher Lao Shu, you too can reap the rewards of Feng Shoe.

L.S./M.W.D.

# FROM THE BOOK OF FENG SHOE:

*If the shoe fits, wear it, but only if they have it in your color.*

# CHAPTER THE FIRST—
# THE BASICS OF FENG SHOE

# FROM THE BOOK OF FENG SHOE:

*The feet of a woman should be comfortable in her shoes; cramped feet and bent toes convert positive energy of the soul to negative energy of the sole.*

# THE FOUR ELEMENTS

Devotees of Feng Shoe should be aware of its four auspicious elements: Wood, Fire, Earth, and Metal. These elements in different combinations can make you feel either footloose or lead you down the foot-path toward enlightenment.

The energy or *ch'i* emanating from each pair of shoes is derived from the material or materials that make up that pair of shoes.

WOOD ENERGY, which tends to be comfortable, but ugly, enhances stability and growth. This energy is obtained from cork or wooden soles. A good example of this type of shoe is the Swedish clog. Do not wear wood shoes on cobblestone streets or on uneven pavement. Do wear them on muddy rural paths.

FIRE ENERGY, residing in shoes that are dressy or the latest thing in fashion, enhances sexiness and creativity. Fire energy reigns supreme in shoes made of satin or peau de soie. Consider wearing such shoes when you have an important business meeting. Do not (and Lao Shu could not have been more explicit on this point) wear them on a first date or when meeting your Internet lover for the first time...you might just be too hot to handle.

**eaRTH eNeRGY,** represented by shoes that we wear on an everyday basis, calms and renews the spirit. This energy is gathered by wearing shoes made of cotton, leather, or any other natural fabric. Unless you wish to live life at an unbearable pace, use these as your default footwear.

**METAL ENERGY** gives the wearer strength, and is very powerful. It is best utilized as an enhancement, such as buckles and designs made of metal thread. Be sparing in your use of metal. You know what heavy metal sounds like; think of that in the guise of a shoe.

# FENG SHOE TIP:

*Don't wear shoes of unnatural materials. In other words, don't wear plastic shoes. Plastic is an artificial substance made of long polymer chains. This allows ch'i to enter the shoe, but the complexity of the atomic structure of the plastic blocks it from exiting the shoe and traveling upward to your center. Too much trapped energy causes the feet to swell and to exude moisture and bromhydrosis (stink foot).*

囍

# CHAPTER THE SECOND—
# SHOE STYLES

# FROM THE BOOK OF FENG SHOE:

*Without the right shoe, nothing is possible.*

# Dress Shoes

are very special. They are the apotheosis of female energy *(yin)* designed to gather male energy *(yang)*. Designed correctly and made with the right materials and colors, they are very powerful shoes. Care must be exercised in choosing them. The following guidelines should help in choosing the proper color for your dress shoes:

**WHILE WHITE** is often thought to be the absence of color, the opposite is actually true. White is the blending of all colors of the spectrum. Therefore, white is to be used in a dress shoe only when all the planets are aligned correctly and the seasons are just right—in June, for a wedding, for example, and only if you're the bride.

囍

# HAPPINESS

I have found true joy.

There is a shop on
my street,

where shoes are half off.

# aDVICE

Dress for success with

expensive designer
clothes . . .

And some killer shoes.

WHITE can be used in an athletic shoe as well. The blending of all colors in white maximizes physical fitness and performance in a full spectrum of activities, from tennis to sex to the L'eggs Half Marathon.

**BLACK** is truly the absence of all colors. This means that black is the perfect color to attract (suck in) all types of energy. With no color to augment or detract from the energy flow, *ch'i* flows unfiltered into the wearer. Lao Shu suggests that you own multiple pairs of black shoes.

**USE RED** to attract men and their fiery *yang* essence. Like moths to a flame, males (propelled by their *yang* energy) are drawn to bright, shiny objects. Red shoes can have this effect even if unseen (if tucked under a bar stool, for example).

Common sense would imply that bringing them into open view (for example, by crossing your legs) could only increase their impact. Thus, if you find yourself wearing red shoes (after coming out of the trance-like state that often attends the choosing of the shoe), you are highly likely, almost certain, to have a good day (or night!).

The correct color, when coordinated to a specific outfit, can enhance the flow of energy throughout the entire body. This can lead to facial flush, witty repartee, and good posture.

# FENG SHOE TIP:

*Shoe of multi-colored stripes or diagonal patterns scatters energy.*

**Translation:** Don't wear plaid shoes (unless, of course, they're Burberry plaid).

# CHAPTER THE THIRD—
# SHOE STORAGE

It is vitally important that shoes be stored properly. Simply throwing them into the closet, or leaving them lying around, will cause them to lose their *ch'i*-gathering abilities. Therefore, shoes need their own special storage spaces.

The Book of Feng Shoe recommends storing shoes in a natural environment, free from outside contamination. With the advent of modern shoe science, many storage items have become available for the followers of Feng Shoe. Some are good; some are bad.

## SHOE TREES

It seems right and fitting to put your shoes on display. A shoe tree is an excellent choice, provided that it is made of a natural substance like wood. Never, never use a plastic shoe tree. With a natural shoe tree, you can make use of your home's Feng Shui as well as enhance your Feng Shoe. Place the shoe trees in the most auspicious corner of your home. Place only shoes of the same style, color, and fabric on neighboring shoe trees. The blending of styles, colors, and fabrics will confuse your shoes' *ch'i* energy and it will take several hours of wearing the shoe after you take it off the tree before the correct energy flow can be achieved.

# PLASTIC SHOE STORAGE APARTMENTS

We've all seen these advertised, usually with the enticement: "Stores 25 pairs of shoes. Hangs conveniently over the door. Made of plastic for easy clean up."

They're ugly and unnatural. Don't insult your shoes by using them.

# SHOE BOXES

Shoes must never be boxed after you purchase them. The box, no matter what it's made of, blocks the energy in the shoe from escaping. There have been reports (so far unsubstantiated) of red, high-heeled dress shoes being kept too long in shoe boxes and exploding.

# SHOE armoires

These are usually made of pressed wood or cardboard and designed to store shoes in your closet. While roomier than shoe boxes, and made of natural (though highly processed and unrecognizable) materials, they are not recommended because, again, they block the energy of the shoes.

# THE PERFECT ENVIRONMENT

Devout followers of Feng Shoe own lots of shoes. Therefore, the shoes must have a room of their own. A spare bedroom is excellent for this purpose; a den will do as well. Do not, however, utilize the basement, the attic, or the garage. There's so much *yang* (male) energy in those places that it could upset the finely tuned energy balance in your shoes.

Further, when storing shoes in their own room, you must make use of the principles of Feng Shui and Feng Shoe. Each basic color and style of shoe has its own area of the room. Mixing shoes while storing is bad Feng Shoe. Red dress shoes should go in the northeast corner of the room. Black dress shoes go in the southeast corner

of the room. White dress shoes go in the northwest corner of the room. Blue dress shoes go in the southwest corner of the room. Red work shoes go in the southeast corner of another room. White work shoes go in the northwest corner of another room . . .

HMMM . . . SIX DIFFERENT STYLES OF SHOE MEANS SIX DIFFERENT ROOMS. . . .

ON SECOND THOUGHT,
YOU'D BETTER MOVE INTO
A BIGGER HOUSE AND
BUY MORE SHOES.

# CHAPTER
# THE FOURTH—
# SHOE SHOPPING

# FROM THE BOOK OF FENG SHOE:

*Wise is the woman who knows the day the new styles go on sale.*

THE MOST AUSPICIOUS
DAYS TO SHOP FOR SHOES
ARE THOSE DAYS THAT
END IN THE LETTER "Y."

SHOE SHOPPING CAN BE
DONE AT ANY TIME OF DAY,
AND IN ANY WEATHER.

SHOE SHOPPING
CAN BE DONE ALONE OR
WITH FRIENDS.

# B

e wary of shoe sales. Most often they are designed to get rid of bad *ch'i* shoes that nobody else would buy at regular prices. You can find good shoes at sales, but it requires effort, planning, and concentration.

## Let Lao Shu's advice guide you:

*Be calm and tactically aware*
*before venturing forth unto the*
*cobbler who bargains.*

Before shoe shopping, calm yourself by meditating in the center of your shoe storage room. Place a woven mat of green sawgrass in the center of the room. Light incense and darken the room. Sit on the mat with your legs crossed. Clear your mind of all extraneous thoughts. Breathe slowly and deeply. Focus your mind on what you hope to accomplish.

## CHANTING IS OPTIONAL.

# POSSIBLE CHANTS:

"DO YOU . . . HAVE THESE . . . IN RED?"

"WILL YOU . . . TAKE ANOTHER 10% OFF . . . IF I BUY . . . TWO PAIR?"

"I SAW . . . THEM FIRST . . . BITCH."

When you feel refreshed, relaxed, and at one with your shoes, go forth and shop.

Scientifically speaking, there is a correct time of day to shop for shoes. Since feet swell as the day wears on, it's best to shop in the late afternoon or early evening. This has the added bonus of giving you an excellent reason to leave work early.

# Braving the Shoe Store.

Do not rush into the shoe store. Browse outside first—window shop. Pretend you are Carrie Bradshaw and the neighborhood shoe store is Gucci. Gauge the quality and selection of shoes from the displays. Glance inside to see the ratio of salespeople to customers. A good ratio is two customers per salesperson. Any higher than that, the salesperson will be too busy to pay adequate attention to your needs.

If all conditions are right, walk slowly into the store. Remain calm. Do not rush. Keep your  elbows relaxed and at your side; you can use them later if things get violent. Study the body language of the other shoppers, à la James Bond. Pause a moment at the front of the store to get a feel for the energy of the shoes. If you are properly attuned, the *ch'i* of the correct pair (or pairs, if you're lucky) of shoes will draw you to them.

Judge the shoes' color, style, and materials. Try the shoes on. Never try on only one shoe; put on both, and walk around for awhile. Feel the flow of energy from the shoes. If the energy is not quite right, ask for the shoe in a different color. Confront the *yin* of the other female shoppers and gauge their reactions. Contact the *yang* of any males in

the store, and revel in any connections that your shoes make with them.

You will know the right shoe when you put it on. Your

feet will immediately bond with the shoes. Peace and happiness will reside in your soul. You will intuitively understand that you and the shoes have become *one*.

There really is no word to describe the feeling of finding the right shoes at the right price—although "orgasmic" does come close. Do not, however, utter any guttural sounds. With the right shoes, you will have that opportunity soon enough.

# CHAPTER THE FIFTH—
# SHOE MAKERS AND THEIR CRAFT

# FROM THE BOOK OF FENG SHOE:

*The higher the heel of the shoe, the closer you are to Heaven's gate.*

althought most of Lao Shu's writings deal with the universal truths of Feng Shoe, Ms. Shu did venture occasionally into diatribes against local shoe makers. For example, of Yun Wa, a local cobbler, she writes: "Do not buy from this merchant. His shoes look bad and they cost too much." However, cost is not always the deciding factor for devotees of Feng Shoe. In the same chapter, she writes: "Blu Zwei makes the finest shoes of the best materials. I will buy them, even if they are expensive."

While Lao Shu mentioned cobblers by name, one can only assume that this was before too many lawyers were around to sue for damages. Today, however, we can't do the same thing and recommend (or warn you against) specific shoe manufacturers.

We can say, however, that there are many fine makers of shoes out there. They range from the very inexpensive to the budget-busters. Any woman worth her weight in shoes knows the names of Prada, Manolo Blahnik, Choo, Weitzman,

Ferragamo, Gucci, Bruno Magli, Chanel, and Spade. And she especially knows the shoe manufacturer that's often mentioned on *Sex and the City* (although for the reasons stated above we cannot specifically recommend that brand).

Therefore, whose shoe to buy becomes a matter of personal choice. But, always bear in mind the wisdom of Lao Shu: "The well-made shoe is a bargain at any price, but, it's a better bargain when half off."

# FENG SHOE TIP:

*Don't keep shoes hoping they will come back into vogue. By the time they do, you'll probably be too old to be wearing that style.*

# CHAPTER THE SIXTH—
# FAMOUS FENG SHOE-ISMS

"AND BEHOLD, ON THE NINTH DAY, AND EVERY HOLIDAY THEREAFTER, THE MERCHANT DID CREATE THE SHOE SALE, AND THE WOMEN OF THE VILLAGE LOOKED UPON IT, AND CALLED IT GOOD."

"IF A WOMAN'S SLIPPERS ARE MADE IN THE LIKENESS OF AN ANIMAL, SHE SHALL BECOME LIKE THAT ANIMAL WHEN WEARING THEM. THEREFORE, BE WARY OF SLIPPERS THAT LOOK LIKE PIGS WHEN THERE IS AN ABUNDANCE OF CHOCOLATE IN THE HOUSE."

"THE COBBLER WHO
DESIGNS UNCOMFORTABLE
SHOES SHALL BE FORCED
TO WEAR THEM AS
PUNISHMENT."

囍

"THE SHOE THAT IS
ON SALE AT A BARGAIN
PRICE HAS NO MORE OR
LESS *CH'I* THAN THE SHOE
AT REGULAR PRICE, BUT
BUYING TWO FOR ONE IS
AN EXCELLENT THING."

# CHAPTER THE SEVENTH—
# SHU-KU

Lao Shu is responsible for creating a very special kind of poetry, based on the ancient art of Japanese Haiku. Since her poems were about shoes rather than the four seasons, however, she chose to call them "Shu-ku."

# LaMeNT

These are perfect shoes.

They match everything
I own.

They don't have my size!

# CONFUSION

Two pair, or just one?

They look so really
good, but

they are not on sale.

# GOING OUT FOR THE EVENING

My hair is a mess,

but my shoes are pretty great.

So, I'm good to go.

# THE
# PERFECT MAN

Not because he's rich

or cute, but because
he knows

how to buy me shoes.

# A FINAL THOUGHT FROM LAO SHU

*When a woman finds her sole-mate, all the portals of happiness open, bliss and contentment fill her soul, and bunions and corns are banished forever.*

HAPPINESS STARTS
WITHIN YOUR SOLE.